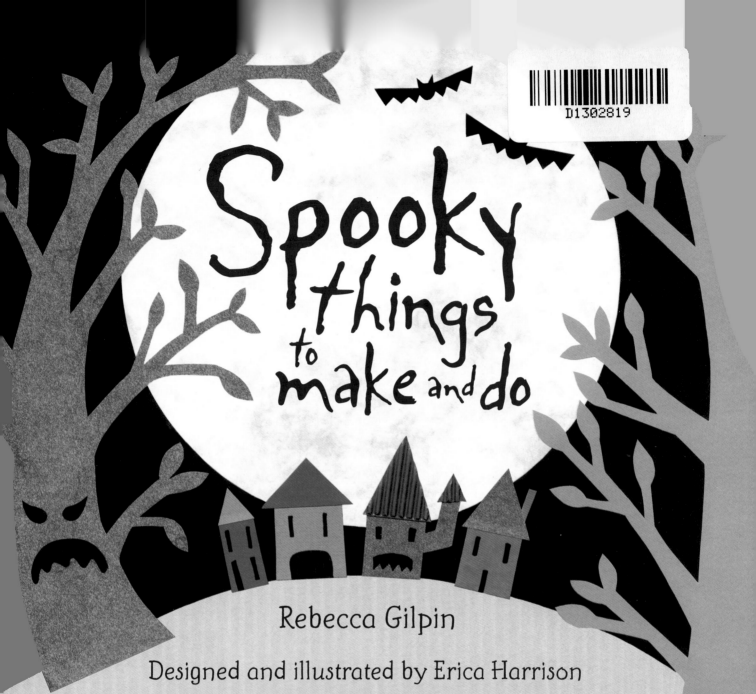

Spooky things to make and do

Rebecca Gilpin

Designed and illustrated by Erica Harrison

Steps illustrated by Jo Moore
Photographs by Howard Allman

Contents

Big slimy eyeball beastie

Pull your finger back to splatter the paint onto the paper.

Blow hard to make the paint run in different directions.

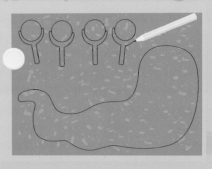

1. Lay a large piece of thick green paper on lots of newspapers. Dip a dry paintbrush into runny light green paint. Pull a finger over the bristles to splatter the paper.

2. To make the eyes, draw around a small lid seven times on white paper. Cut out the circles. One at a time, blob runny red paint onto a circle and blow it with a straw.

3. When the green paint is dry, draw a slimy shape on the paper. Draw around the lid four times, and draw eye stalks around each circle, like this. Cut out the shapes.

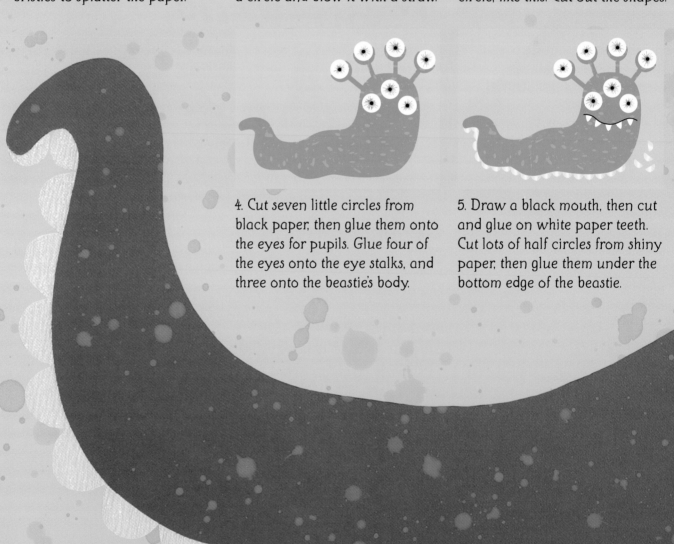

4. Cut seven little circles from black paper, then glue them onto the eyes for pupils. Glue four of the eyes onto the eye stalks, and three onto the beastie's body.

5. Draw a black mouth, then cut and glue on white paper teeth. Cut lots of half circles from shiny paper, then glue them under the bottom edge of the beastie.

You could add drips of *slime* cut from shiny paper.

This background paper was splattered with different shades of green paint.

flapping bat

Make the rectangle a little longer than your hand.

1. Cut a rectangle from thin cardboard. Draw a bat's head and body, then add ears and feet. Cut out the bat, then erase any pencil lines.

To make a bat with a patterned body, glue patterned paper onto the cardboard before you draw the shape.

Draw a curve on one side of the wing and points on the other side.

2. Fold another piece of cardboard in half. Then, draw a wing about the same length as the bat. Holding the layers together, cut out the wings.

3. Using a hole puncher, carefully punch a hole on each side of the bat's body in the position shown above. Then, make a hole at the top of each wing, too.

Make the holes close together.

4. Move the hole puncher a little way around the curved side of one of the wings, then make a second hole. Make a hole in the other wing in the same way.

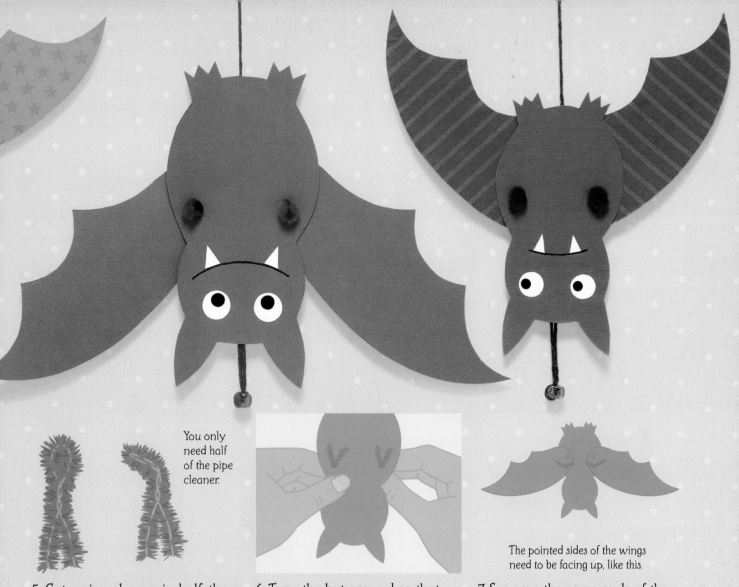

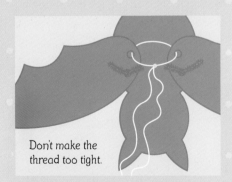

You only need half of the pipe cleaner.

The pointed sides of the wings need to be facing up, like this.

5. Cut a pipe cleaner in half, then cut one piece in half again. Bend the shorter pieces in the middle, and twist them. Bend the twisted part of each one over, like this.

6. Turn the bat around so that the head is at the bottom. Then, push the twisted ends of the pipe cleaners through the holes in the body, like this.

7. Squeeze the open ends of the pipe cleaners together, then thread on the wings through the bottom holes. Open out the ends again and gently press them flat.

Don't make the thread too tight.

When you pull the thread, the wings flap up.

8. Cut a long piece of thread and push it through the holes in the top of the wings. Then, tie the thread in a knot, in the gap between the wings, like this.

9. Thread a bead onto the end of the thread and tie it on. To make a loop for hanging the bat, fold another piece of thread in half and tape it between the feet.

10. Draw eyes on white paper, cut them out and glue them on. Draw a mouth and add fangs. Hang up the bat, then gently pull the bead to make the wings flap.

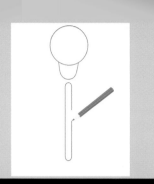

1. Lay a small plate near the top of a large piece of cardboard and draw around it. Add a jaw below the circle, then draw a long sausage for a spine.

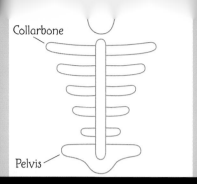

Collarbone

Pelvis

2. Draw shapes for a collarbone a little way down from the top of the spine. Add four ribs below the collarbone, and a pelvis at the bottom of the spine, like this.

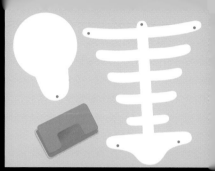

3. Cut around the outline of the shapes. Then, using a hole puncher, make holes in the skull, spine, collarbone and pelvis, shown by the red dots above.

Trim the ends of the thread.

4. To join the head and body, cut a piece of white thread. Push it through the hole in the bottom of the skull and the hole in the spine, then knot it, like this.

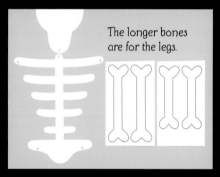

The longer bones are for the legs.

5. Fold two pieces of thin white cardboard in half. On one piece, draw two bones about the length of the spine. Draw two shorter bones on the other piece.

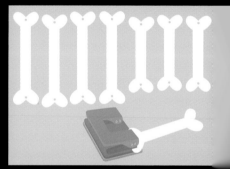

6. Keeping the cardboard folded, cut around the bones, to make four long bones and four shorter ones. Then, punch holes near the ends of all the bones, like this.

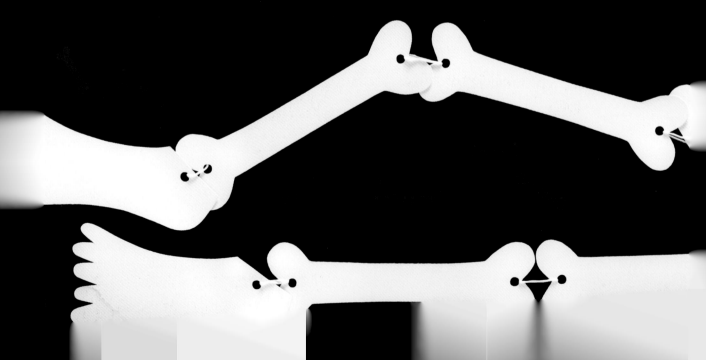

You can move your skeleton's arms and legs into lots of different positions.

7. To make the arms, join two of the shorter bones with a piece of thread, as before. Join the other two short bones, too. Then, join both arms onto the collarbone.

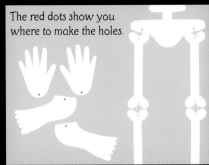

The red dots show you where to make the holes.

8. Join the long bones to make legs and join them onto the pelvis. Then, draw hands and feet on scraps of cardboard, cut them out and punch holes in them.

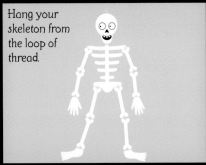

Hang your skeleton from the loop of thread.

9. Join the hands and feet onto the arms and legs. Using a black felt-tip pen, draw a face on the skull. Then, tape a loop of thread onto the back of the skull.

Creepy sliding eyes portrait

Punch one eye at a time.

1. Cut out a square of white cardboard, then cut a strip off the top, like this. Then, use a hole puncher to make holes for eyes, in the bigger piece.

2. Lay the edges of the two pieces of cardboard together again. Then, press lots of pieces of sticky tape along the join, but don't tape over the eye holes.

3. Turn the cardboard over. Using a pencil and a ruler, draw a picture frame. Then, using the holes for the eyes, draw a creepy portrait inside the frame.

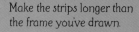
Make the strips longer than the frame you've drawn.

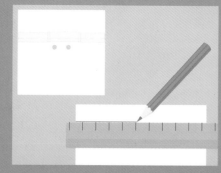

4. Fill in the portrait with felt-tip pens, then outline it with a black pen. To make the frame, cut four strips from gold cardboard. Make one side of each strip wobbly.

5. Trim two of the cardboard strips so that they fit down the sides of the frame. Glue them on, then cut strips for the top and bottom and glue them on, too.

6. Turn the picture over. Then, to make a strip for the sliding eyes, lay a ruler across a piece of cardboard, like this. Draw along the ruler, then cut along the line.

8

For a gallery, draw lots of spooky people along a long piece of cardboard and paint the wall around them before you glue on the frames.

You could draw someone running away from the creepy portraits, too.

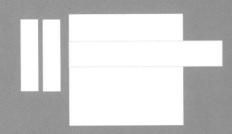

7. Lay the cardboard strip over the eye holes, with one end touching the left-hand edge of the picture. Then, cut two short strips of cardboard.

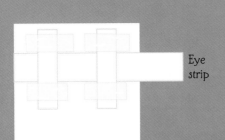

Eye strip

8. Lay the strips across the eye strip, in the positions shown above. Then, attach them with sticky tape as close to the eye strip as you can.

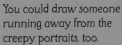

Leave a gap here.   Don't leave a gap on this side.

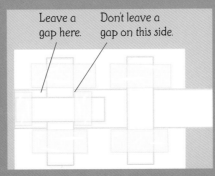

9. Then, cut another short strip of cardboard. Tape it on like this, leaving a gap on the left-hand side. This lets you slide the eye strip from side to side.

10. Turn the picture over again. Draw a spot in the right-hand side of each eye hole for a pupil. Then, slide the eye strip from side to side and watch the eyes move.

Spooky sunset castle painting

1. For the sunset sky behind the castle, pour some thick yellow paint onto an old plate. Then, pour thick orange and red paints onto the plate, too.

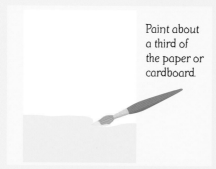

Paint about a third of the paper or cardboard.

2. Dip a large paintbrush into the yellow paint. Then, paint a thick stripe across the bottom of a large piece of thick paper or thin cardboard, like this.

3. Without washing your brush, dip it into the orange paint. Starting at the top of the yellow stripe, paint an orange stripe that blends into the yellow one.

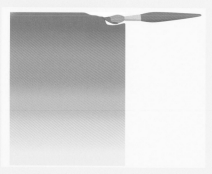

4. Without washing your brush, dip it into the red paint. Add a stripe at the top of the paper, blending the red paint into the orange paint, as before.

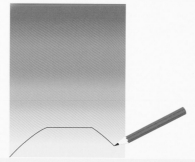

5. Leave all of the paint to dry completely. Then, use a pencil to draw a rounded hill with a flat top at the bottom of the paper, like this.

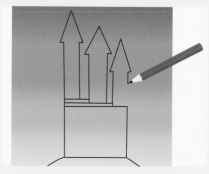

6. Draw a rectangle for a castle on the flat top of the hill. Add two very thin rectangles along the top, then draw three tall towers with pointed roofs.

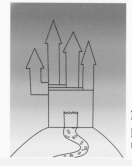

Draw little pebbles on the path.

7. Draw another tower, coming from the side of the castle, then draw a doorway at the bottom. Then, draw a winding path going down the hill.

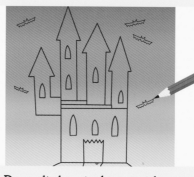

8. Draw little windows with pointed tops on the towers. Draw some on the main part of the castle, too. Then, add lots of bats flying around the castle.

9. Using a paintbrush, fill in the castle, hill and bats with thick black paint. Use a thin brush to fill in the fiddly bits if you need to. Then, leave the paint to dry.

If you have a silver
pen, you could draw
shiny eyes on the bats.

The windows and
door on this part
of the castle look
like a spooky face.

Floating ghosts

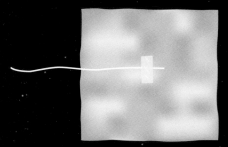

1. Cut a large square of kitchen foil, then cut a long piece of string to hang the ghost from. Tape one end of the string onto the middle of the foil, like this.

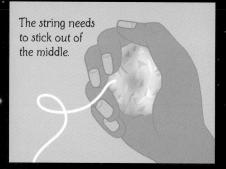

The string needs to stick out of the middle.

2. Roughly scrunch the foil around the string, to make a ball for the ghost's head. Then, squeeze the ball to make it as round and smooth as you can.

You could make ghosts with different expressions.

Lay the string out to one side.

3. Rip lots of small pieces from white tissue paper. Then, lay the foil ball on a piece of plastic foodwrap. Brush part of the ball with white glue.

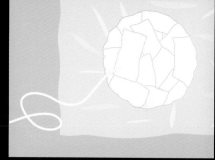

4. Press pieces of tissue paper onto the wet glue. Then, cover the rest of the ball with tissue paper in the same way. Leave the glue to dry completely.

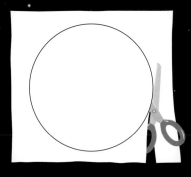

5. While the glue dries, use a felt-tip pen to draw around a dinner plate on a piece of thin white material. Then, cut out the circle, just inside the line.

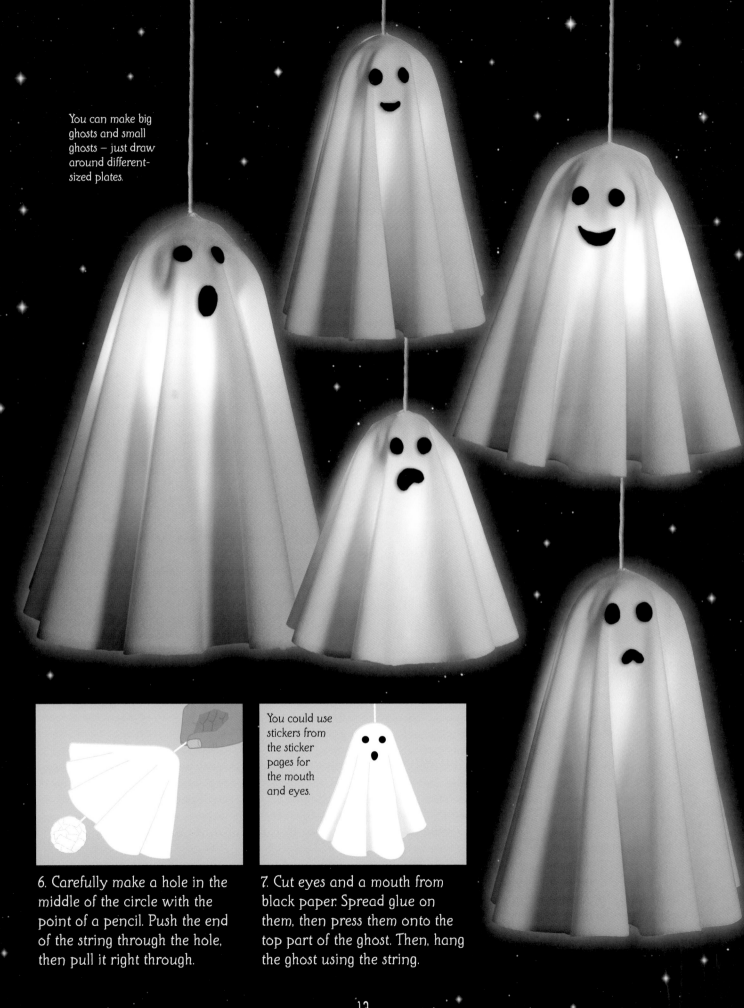

You can make big ghosts and small ghosts – just draw around different-sized plates.

You could use stickers from the sticker pages for the mouth and eyes.

6. Carefully make a hole in the middle of the circle with the point of a pencil. Push the end of the string through the hole, then pull it right through.

7. Cut eyes and a mouth from black paper. Spread glue on them, then press them onto the top part of the ghost. Then, hang the ghost using the string.

13

Monster in the forest

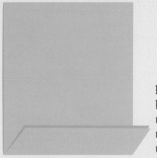

Fold both layers of the paper to make the flaps.

1. To make a monster, fold a long rectangle of thick blue paper in half, with its short ends together. Fold the bottom up to make flaps for the base, then unfold it again.

Make the horns and fingertips touch the fold, too.

2. Draw an arch for the body above the flap, making the middle of it touch the fold at the top of the paper. Then, add two horns and two arms.

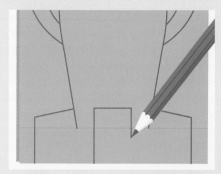

3. Draw a foot on each side of the body, above the flap. Then, draw lines down from the feet to the bottom of the flap. Add a rectangle between the legs, too.

Don't cut along the parts shown here in red.

4. Carefully cut out the monster with scissors, making sure that you don't cut all the way along the fold at the top. Then, erase any remaining pencil lines.

Use a thin paintbrush.

5. Using a black pen, draw two eyes, eyebrows and a big gaping mouth. Paint the horns with white paint and add pointed teeth, then let the paint dry.

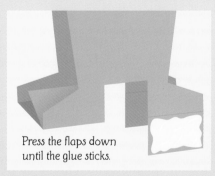

Press the flaps down until the glue sticks.

6. For the base, spread glue on the flaps at the front of the monster. Fold both these flaps back and press them onto the flaps on the other side of the body.

7. To make a tree, fold a piece of green paper and make flaps for the base, as you did in step 1. Then, draw a tree trunk above the flap.

8. Add lots of branches and twigs above the trunk, making several of them touch the fold at the top. Then, draw lines down from the trunk to the bottom of the flap.

9. Cut out the tree without cutting through the twigs along the fold. Then, fold and glue the flaps to make the base, as you did in step 6.

To make a pointed tree, make sure that the point at the top touches the fold in the paper.

You could make little monsters from smaller pieces of paper.

15

Scuttling rat

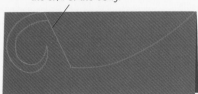

Draw a straight line for the end of the body.

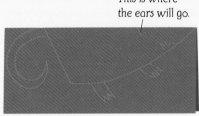

This is where the ears will go.

Don't spread glue on the body.

1. Fold a rectangle of thick brown paper in half. With the fold at the top, draw a curved shape for a rat's body. Then, add a curving tail, starting at the fold.

2. Draw a mouth with spikes for teeth, then add two feet on the rat's body. Draw a short line down from the fold for the ears. Then, carefully cut out the rat.

3. Unfold the rat and erase any lines. Then, to glue the two halves of its tail together, spread glue on one of the tails. Fold the rat in half and press the tails together.

To make a rat sit up, bend the tail out to one side, so that it lies flat.

4. Draw a nose and eyes on the rat. Then, fold another piece of brown paper in half for the ears. Draw a rounded ear against the fold, then cut out the shape.

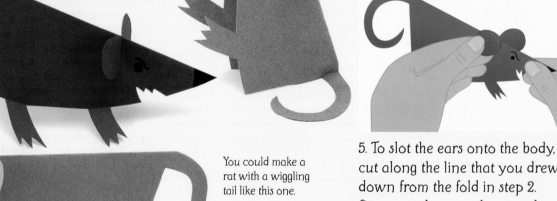

You could make a rat with a wiggling tail like this one.

5. To slot the ears onto the body, cut along the line that you drew down from the fold in step 2. Open out the ears, then gently push them into the slot.

16

Ghastly ghost

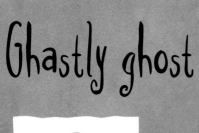

1. Pressing very lightly with a pencil, draw a curve for a ghost's head on a piece of white tissue paper. Then, add two wobbly arms and a curving body.

The glue soaks through the tissue paper and sticks the ghost down.

2. Cut out the shape, just inside the line. Then, lay it on a piece of blue paper. Brush white glue all over the ghost, making sure that you don't rip the tissue paper.

Use a thin paintbrush.

3. Let the glue dry. Then, paint two round eyes on the ghost with thick black paint. Add a gaping mouth, then leave the paint to dry completely.

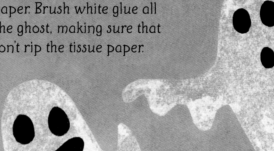

You could fill a big piece of paper with lots of ghosts with different expressions.

You can make baby ghosts from scraps of white tissue paper.

Toothy monster-mouth bag

1. Draw a line across a paper carrier bag, below the bottom of the handles. Then, cut along the line to make two pieces, like this. You don't need the top piece.

2. To make a new handle, place one hand near the top of the bag, with your fingers together. Then, draw a little mark on either side of your hand, like this.

3. Draw a curved shape for a monster's mouth, using the little pencil marks as the ends of the mouth. Add pointed teeth along the bottom edge of the mouth.

Put your hand through the monster's mouth to carry the bag.

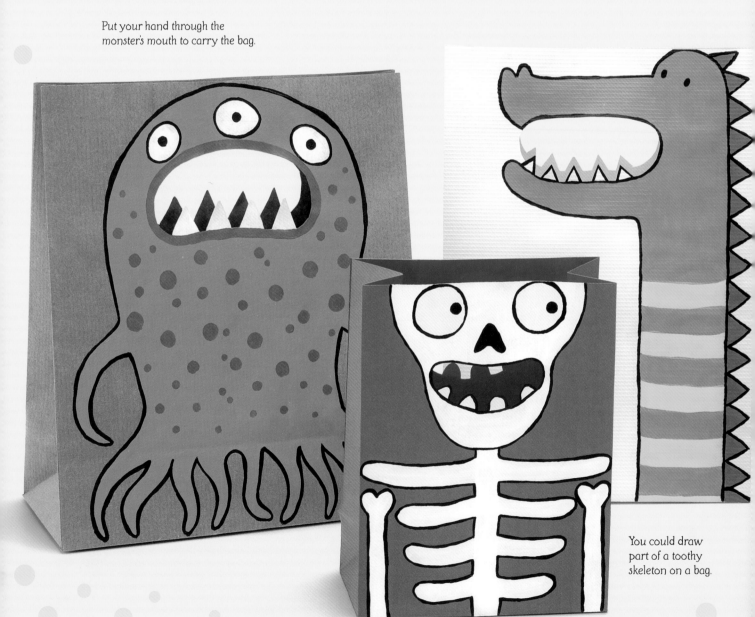

You could draw part of a toothy skeleton on a bag.

4. Before you draw the rest of the monster, fold the flap at the bottom of the bag to the back. Then, draw an arch over the mouth for the monster's head.

5. Draw a curved arm on each side of the monster, then add lots of tentacles at the bottom. Draw three round eyes above the mouth, too.

6. To make a hole for the handle, very carefully push the point of a sharp pencil through the middle of the mouth. Push it through both layers of the bag.

Monsters don't have to have teeth – try drawing a scary ghost with a gaping mouth instead.

7. Push one blade of a pair of scissors through the hole. Then, holding both layers of the bag together, carefully cut around the monster's mouth.

You could paint spots on your monster.

8. Lay the bag on a newspaper, then fill in the monster with thick paints. When the paint is dry, outline the monster with a black pen. Draw around his eyes, too.

Sinister spiders

The lines need to go across the oval, like this.

1. To make the spider's body, lay a piece of corrugated cardboard with the lines going across. Then, draw an oval about the size of a bar of soap on the cardboard.

2. Cut out the oval, then push four pipecleaners through the zigzag gaps inside the cardboard. Push them through until the legs on each side are equal lengths.

3. Gently scrunch a large piece of kitchen foil until it is about the same size as the oval. Squash the foil until the top is smooth, then glue it onto the oval, like this.

You could bend the ends of the spider's legs out to make feet.

To make a little spider,
cut a smaller oval for
the body and trim
off the ends of the
pipecleaners.

Cover
the gaps
between the
legs, too.

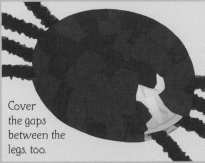

You could use eye
and fang stickers from
the sticker pages.

4. Bend the legs out a little, then lay the spider on a piece of plastic foodwrap. Rip lots of strips from black tissue paper and put them onto a newspaper.

5. Brush a strip of tissue paper with white glue, then press it onto the spider's body. Press on lots more strips of tissue paper, until the whole body is covered.

6. To make the spider stand up, bend each leg into a curve. Cut eyes and fangs from white paper and glue them on. Then, add black dots in the middle of the eyes.

Pop-up vampire card

1. For the card, cut two rectangles the same size from two shades of thick paper. Fold both of the rectangles in half, with the short edges together.

Make both of the cuts the same length.

2. Make two small cuts into the fold in one of the rectangles, to make a flap. Crease the fold to the front, like this. Fold it over to the back, then unfold it again.

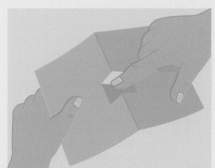

3. Open up the card and push the flap through the middle of the fold, like this. Then, close the card, with the flap inside, and smooth it flat.

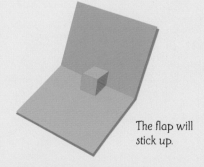

The flap will stick up.

4. Open out the card again. Spread glue on the back of the card with the flap, but don't glue the flap. Press it onto the other card, lining up the folds.

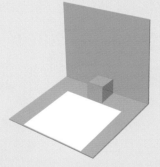

5. For the vampire, cut a square of thick white paper that fits inside the card, like this. If the vampire is this size, he won't show when the card is closed.

Draw a mouth with pointed fangs.

6. Draw the vampire's head and body with outstretched arms. Draw his legs and feet, then add his clothes. Fill him in with felt-tip pens, then cut him out.

7. Lay the vampire on a piece of tissue paper and draw a large rectangle for his cape. Make it the same height as the vampire and twice as wide as his arms.

8. Cut out the cape. Hold it a quarter of the way down and twist it, then press the twisted part flat. Then, brush white glue all over the back of the vampire.

You could make a card with a witch wearing a black cape.

Spread glue on the front of the flap and press the vampire's legs onto it.

9. Press the vampire onto the cape, so that his arms are glued along the top edge of the paper. Then, glue the vampire onto the front of the flap on the card.

10. Using felt-tip pens, draw bats on a piece of white paper. Cut them out and glue them onto the back of the card, behind the vampire. Let the glue dry.

Creepy creatures of the deep

1. For a creepy squid creature, draw an oval on a piece of paper. Draw four tentacles, then add more tentacles in between them. Add a creepy face.

2. Mix thick pale blue paint, then paint the creature's head. Fill in the first four tentacles that you drew, too. Then, paint the other tentacles a darker shade of blue.

Don't fill in the eyes and mouth.

3. Paint two eyebrows, then add black dots in the eyes for pupils. Fill in the mouth, leaving the teeth white. Then, paint spots on the head with very pale blue paint.

You could paint a whole deep-sea scene like this one, filled with lots of creepy squid and jelly creatures.

Try adding some curling, clutching weeds when you paint the bubbles.

Draw the jelly creature a little way from the squid creature.

Use a white pencil.

4. Draw a curved shape for a deep-sea jelly creature, then add a scary mouth with fangs. Paint the creature pale pink, but don't paint the mouth or fangs.

5. When the paint is dry, add eyebrows with bright pink paint. Use a black felt-tip pen to draw the eyes and mouth, then draw around the white fangs, too.

6. Carefully paint the sea around the creatures with dark paint. Add air bubbles with lilac paint. When the paint is dry, draw tentacles on the jelly creature.

Zombie march

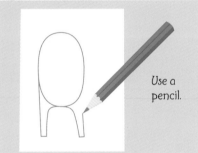

Use a pencil.

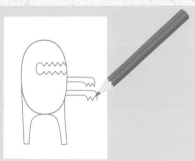

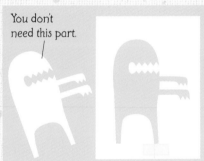

You don't need this part.

1. To make a stencil for a zombie, draw an oval for the body on a rectangle of thick paper. Then, add two legs at the bottom of the zombie's body.

2. Draw a mouth with jagged teeth about a third of the way down the body. Draw two arms sticking out, and add claws at the end of them, like this.

3. Using scissors, cut up from the bottom of the paper, as far as the zombie. Carefully cut around it. Then, press a little piece of sticky tape over the cut at the bottom.

To make a zombie march, print lots of zombies facing in the same direction.

You could paint stripes or spots on a zombie when the paint has dried.

4. To print the zombie, lay the stencil on a piece of paper. Spread some thick paint on an old plate, then dip a sponge into the paint.

5. Dab paint all over the hole. Then, lift off the stencil and leave the paint to dry. Add eyes with white and black paints or press on stickers from the sticker pages.

Frankenstein's monster mask

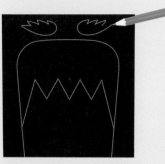

Make the green shape as wide as your face.

1. For the headband, cut a strip of thin cardboard that fits once around your head, with a little overlap. Overlap the ends and secure them with sticky tape.

2. Draw a large shape for the monster's forehead on thin green cardboard. Cut it out, then lay it on a piece of thin black cardboard and draw around it.

3. Lift off the green shape. Then, draw a zigzag for hair inside the outline on the black cardboard. Add two bushy eyebrows. Then, cut out the hair and eyebrows.

To make a Dracula mask, draw a point in the middle of the hair, and add pointed ears instead of bolts.

4. Glue the hair onto the green shape. Then, glue the eyebrows at the bottom, overlapping the edge. Draw two curving wrinkles with a dark green pen.

You could draw the bolts on the scraps from step 3.

5. Draw two chunky T-shaped bolts on a piece of thin dark cardboard. Cut them both out, then fold over the end of each bolt to make a tab, like this.

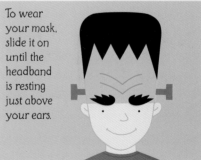

To wear your mask, slide it on until the headband is resting just above your ears.

6. Lay the mask face down. Spread a line of glue along the bottom edge, then press the headband onto it. Then, glue the bolts onto the headband, too.

Spooky full-moon picture

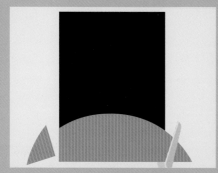

Use a blue chalk if you don't have a chalk pastel.

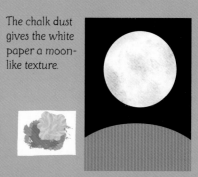

The chalk dust gives the white paper a moon-like texture.

1. Cut a curved shape for a hill from purple paper and glue it at the bottom of a large piece of black paper. Then, trim the sides that overlap the edges.

2. For the moon, draw around a bowl on white paper, then cut out the circle. Make blue chalk dust by scribbling hard with a chalk pastel on a scrap of paper.

3. Scrunch up a small piece of tissue paper. Dip it into the chalk dust, then dab it over the paper moon. Then, glue the moon onto the black paper, above the hill.

4. Using a pencil, draw a curving tree with branches and leaves on blue paper. Draw a second tree on purple paper, then carefully cut out both trees.

5. Glue on the trees so that they overlap the moon and hill. Leave a space for houses in the middle. Then, trim off any parts of the trees that overlap the edges.

6. Draw some wonky rectangles and funny shapes for houses on scraps of blue and purple paper. Cut them out, then glue them along the top of the hill, like this.

7. Cut triangles for roofs from scraps of paper and cardboard and glue them on. Then, draw sinister faces on the blue tree and the houses with a black pen.

8. Using a pencil, draw spooky monsters and bats on pieces of black paper. Cut them all out, then glue the monsters on the hill and the bats on the moon.

9. Draw four round eyes and two speech bubbles on scraps of paper. Cut them all out and glue them onto the picture. Then, write monster talk in the bubbles.

Marzipan skulls

You will need:
a 200g (7oz) block of 'white' marzipan*
red food dye
toothpicks

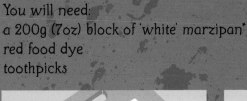

Make the top corners rounded too.

1. Using a knife, carefully cut the block of marzipan in half. Cut it in half again, to make four pieces. Then, cut each piece in half again, to make eight pieces.

2. Using your fingers, shape each piece into a chunky rectangle. Then, squeeze the lower part of each one to make a chin. Make the edges as smooth as you can.

Dip the toothpick into the dye again and again.

3. Using the handle of a wooden spoon, press two eye sockets into each skull, like this. Then, use a toothpick to press in a nose and mouth, too.

4. Pour a few drops of red food dye onto an old plate. Dip the toothpick into the dye, then dab it into the eyes, nose and mouth until they are really red.

You could use blue and green food dye, too.

Try giving each of your skulls a different-shaped mouth.

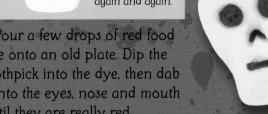

* Marzipan contains ground nuts, so don't give the skulls to anyone who is allergic to nuts.

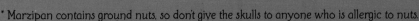

Series editor Fiona Watt • Photographic manipulation by John Russell.
This edition published in 2011, Usborne Publishing Ltd, Usborne House, 83-85 Saffron Hill, London, EC1N 8RT. www.usborne.com
Copyright © 2011, 2007 Usborne Publishing Ltd. The name Usborne and the devices ♀♡ are Trademarks of Usborne Publishing Ltd.
UE First published in America 2007. Printed in Malaysia.